Foreword

In the past, most people saw 'investing' as something other people did. As Ireland grows wealthier more people will have to make decisions about how to manage their money – decisions that may have a substantial effect on their future.

'Investment Advice for Life' is an updated compilation of the much-praised articles published in 1997 and 1998 by the Irish Independent and Bank of Ireland Asset Management. The series opens up the investment choices available to investors in a clear and uncomplicated way and takes you through all the major choices now available.

Cyril Hardiman

Business Correspondent
Irish Independent

Contents

I. Introduction

For the absolute beginner, we start out by answering the basic questions – what can I invest in? What are the risks and possible returns? When should I save and when should I make a longer-term investment?

II. The basics

This section concentrates on the different types of investment that are available and will take you through the pros and cons of each for Irish investors.

III. More about investing

This section looks at some of the ways you can go about investing and takes a brief look at taxation and regulation.

IV. More about the stock market

In periods of lower interest rates such as now, the stock market will probably have a greater role to play in the decisions that Irish investors will make. Part IV gives you a more in-depth understanding of stock markets.

V. Tips about making your mind up

This section will help you decide what type of investor you are and the investments most suited to your circumstances and long-term goals.

Part I

Introduction

for absolute beginners

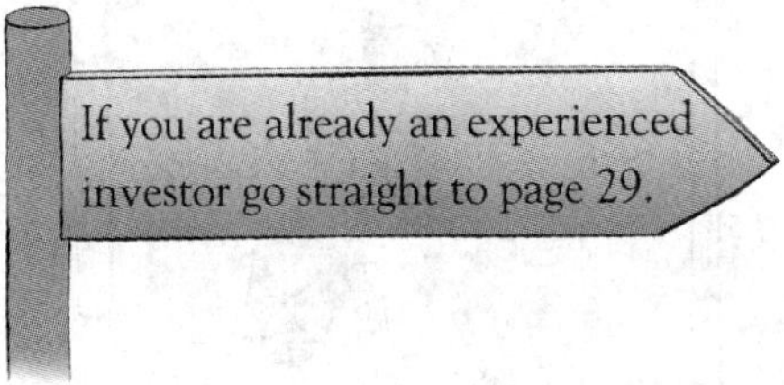

Start
1

Chapter 1

Getting started

Investing wisely is the surest way to provide you and your family with future financial security – but where do you start?

With many commentators suggesting that lower interest rates are more likely in the future, making the right investments is now more important than ever before.

Please note:

Investment performance figures referred to throughout the book are based on historical performance. Readers should note that past performance is no guarantee of what will happen in the future.

A few tips to get you started

What's the difference between short-term and long-term investing?

Short-term investing covers your day-to-day needs and projects you may wish to undertake in the next one to two years. It takes many forms, including deposits and savings bonds – which are ideal if you need access to your money in the short term.

Long-term investing is designed to provide you with investment choices if you don't need access to your money for at least five years. In return for this commitment you can expect to achieve superior growth.

If you think you'll need access to your money, consider this before you invest:

The extent to which you can access your money varies considerably. Some deposit accounts, managed funds and shares can give you almost daily access. Others, such as property and tracker bonds, for example, tend to be less accessible.

Secure returns are a good idea but make sure you know what they're costing you:

For many investors knowing the return they can expect from their investment is essential. However, history shows that the best returns tend to be consistently achieved by investors who are prepared to do without security. This is demonstrated in the chart on page 11, where an investment in a managed fund has significantly outperformed a shorter-term, more secure deposit, in the long run. Of course, the managed fund offered less security than the deposit and there were ups and downs on the way.

Remember, in a low interest rate environment, deposits and other secure homes for your money may not perform as well as they have in the past. But also remember, long-term risk investments are not as secure.

Figure 1: Short and long-term investments compared

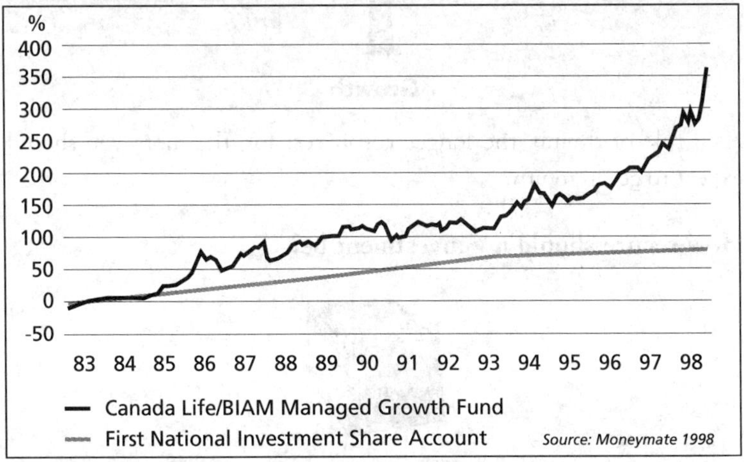

Note: *This graph is based on an investment of IR£10,000 from April 1983 to April 1998. The Canada Life/BIAM Managed Fund is a unit-linked fund. Performance is quoted in Irish Pounds on an offer to bid basis. Investors should note that past performance is not necessarily a guide to future returns. The value of units may fall as well as rise. Up-front charges will apply. Investors may get back less than they originally invested. The deposit used is a First National Investment Share Account over the same period.*

So, what kind of investor are you?

If you are not sure, ask yourself the following questions:

How much can I expect my investment to grow in the long run?

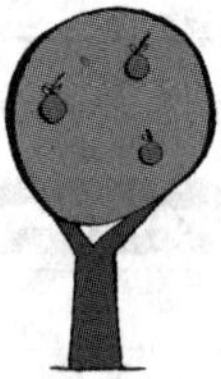

Growth

As a rule of thumb, the longer you invest for, the more you should expect to get in return.

How secure should my investment be?

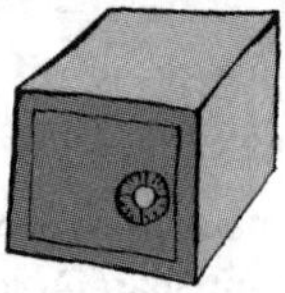

Security

As a rule of thumb, choosing a secure return on your investment means reducing the long-term potential return on your money.

How easy will it be to get at my money once I've invested?

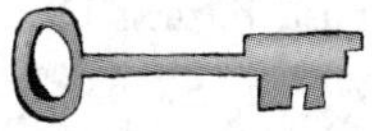

Access

With many types of investment, you can get access to your money on a weekly, if not daily, basis. However, we recommend that you think in terms of investing for five years or more. Any long-term investment may need at least this length of time to get through some ups and downs and start delivering decent returns.

Understanding the investment building blocks

Behind almost every investment you'll find one or a combination of four key ingredients (known in the business as 'asset classes'). These are:

- Cash
- Equities
- Bonds
- Property

We will talk about the characteristics of each of these and will examine each in greater detail, later in the book.

Cash

Cash is quite simply your deposit account, paying an interest rate over a particular period. In the past, returns have varied depending on the interest rate environment.

Historically, returns from cash have been just ahead of inflation over longer terms.

Cash: Investment characteristics

Growth 

Access* 

Security 

**Access may be more restricted with longer term deposits.*

Equities

Equities, also known as shares, give you part ownership in a company.

Historically, high quality equities have tended to be the best-performing of all investment types. The ability of equities to provide top-level performance comes at a price: equities also tend to go up and down in value more than any other type of investment.

Equities: Investment characteristics

Growth 

Access 

Security* 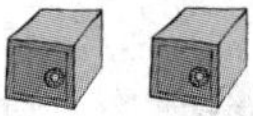

**Individual shares may be significantly riskier.*

Bonds

Bonds are issued by governments and large companies. In return for investing, you get a fixed income and your money back at the end of a specific period. Unlike deposits, you can buy and sell bonds on the stock exchange in the same way as shares. In terms of the returns bonds have achieved in the past, they have often done better than cash but not as well as equities.

Bonds: Investment characteristics

Growth 

Access* 

Security** 

**Access can be much greater than indicated, but at the cost of reduced capital security.*
***Security may vary, depending on the creditworthiness of the issuer of the bond.*

Property

With the highest home ownership rates in the world, Ireland is very familiar with property as an investment.

Property has traditionally performed better than cash in the long run but, in general, has not kept up with equities, although it has performed better in many years. Property investors, however, can often benefit from tax incentives, which supplement the returns.

On the down side, property tends to be relatively 'illiquid' as an investment, i.e. it cannot be bought and sold as quickly as other investments. Lastly, although property has been on an upward trend in Ireland over recent years, it can also go down in value.

Property: Investment characteristics

Growth 

Access 

Security 

These four building blocks are the raw ingredients for almost all long-term investments. From now on, we will refer to these building blocks as 'asset classes'.

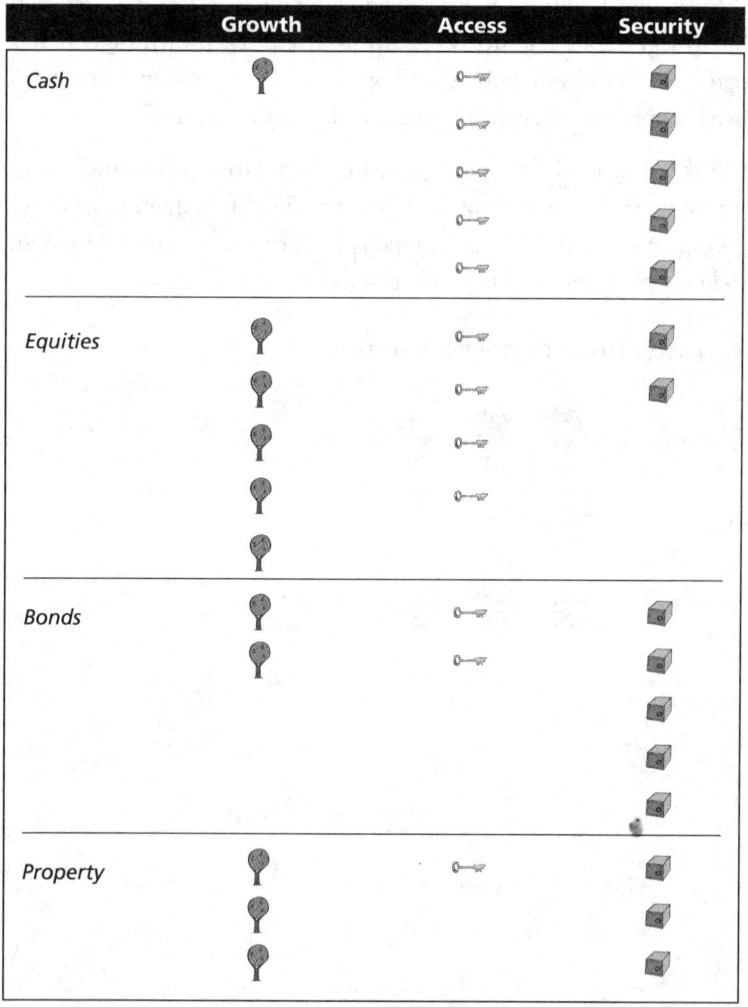

Shares
Bonds
Stocks

Chapter 2

The long and the short of saving and investing

The short term

Usually, short-term saving has an immediate goal, such as a holiday, Christmas or even a wedding. The time frame is less than five years and the amount involved is typically less than IR£10,000.

The long term

If you are planning to invest for the longer term, your time frame will be five years or more, and your objective will probably be a major event – such as your retirement, your children's education, or mortgage repayment. However, some long-term investors do not have a specific goal but simply invest to provide security for their future.

Nearly everyone has a need to do a certain amount of saving and investing. Let's look at both of them, in a little more detail.

Your short-term savings

- Have you any rainy day savings or an emergency fund?
- Are you happy with where you are living/renting at present?
- Have you put money aside this year for holidays and Christmas?

If you answered 'no' to any of these, you might think of increasing your savings.

The question remains, how much can you afford to save? There's no easy way around this: you simply have to sit down and work out your household budget. On page 23, there's a sample worksheet that you can use to get started.

Monthly incomings/outgoings		
A: TOTAL INCOME AFTER TAX		£
Food:		
Housing:	Mortgage/rent	
Utilities:	Electricity	
	Gas	
	Oil	
	Telephone	
Insurance/other financial:		
	House	
	Contents	
	Life	
	Motor	
	Health	
	Mortgage	
	Pension	
Travel & related expenses:		
	Car	
	Public	
Loans:	Credit cards	
	Personal loans	
Other:	Clothing	
	Education	
	Household goods	
	Child care	
B: TOTAL EXPENSES		£
INCOME LEFT OVER (A-B)		£
Amount for saving		
	Christmas	
	Holidays	
	Rainy days	

Your longer-term investments

Most of us are already long-term investors in some shape or form, whether we're aware of it or not. What's more, you don't need a lump sum to be an investor; many investors make smaller regular investments. Some 40 per cent of Irish people invest in their home through a mortgage, while over 50 per cent of us have some kind of pension plan. As you can see from these examples, investing is about the 'big things' in life: your home, your retirement, your children's future. All these big items will cost a great deal more than the average holiday or Christmas presents! To provide a retirement income of IR£15,000, a typical person needs to have built up a fund worth over IR£250,000 based on present interest rates*.

Building up a fund worth that much requires much more growth than the average deposit savings account can produce – especially if you consider how low interest rates are at present.

That's why investing means putting your money into assets that have the scope to grow significantly in value over the longer term.

In the long run, the assets that have tended to be the best at producing superior long-term returns are high quality company shares. The evidence for this has been around for a very long time.

**This estimate is based on the cost of a typical retirement annuity for a male retiring at age 65, providing an income of IR£15,000 p.a. indexed at 5% p.a. This is subject to change depending on the prevailing interest rate environment.*

The Long-Term Returns Table

Throughout this book, we will be referring to the performance of different asset classes in our 'Long-Term Returns Table'.

To estimate their performance, we have used returns from selected indices, as measured in a paper published by Pat Healy for the Society of Actuaries in Ireland in 1996 and updated by BIAM in 1998.

Irish equities are measured by the RIADA Total Return Index as measured by RIADA stockbrokers. Property is measured by the JLW Total Return Index as measured by Jones Lang Wootton.

Bond returns are measured by the RIADA 15 year Index.

Cash returns are measured by the three month DIBOR rate (DIBOR is the Dublin Interbank Offer Rate, the highest deposit rate available).

These index returns do not reflect the performance of individual funds, shares, bonds or properties which could be higher or lower.

> Remember, past performance is no guarantee of future returns.

TABLE 1: THE LONG-TERM RETURNS TABLE

Annual returns from Irish asset classes (before taxes and charges) 1966 to 1997

	Cash	Bonds	Property	Equities	Inflation
30 yrs	10.5%	11.6%	n/a	16.7%	8.2%
25 yrs	11.1%	13.2%	14.2%	16.4%	8.4%
20 yrs	11.1%	13.4%	14.2%	18.2%	6.5%
15 yrs	9.8%	14.6%	10.4%	22.5%	3.8%
10 yrs	8.4%	12.4%	13.4%	18.3%	2.6%
5 yrs	6.6%	14.1%	16.3%	29.7%	2.0%

The table (above) describes the returns achieved by various asset classes from 1966 to 1997, as measured in a paper produced for The Society of Actuaries in Ireland in 1996, updated by BIAM in 1998. Returns do not reflect any charges or taxes which would reduce the returns.

The Long-Term Returns Table will be referred to throughout the book. The table below indicates the level of these returns after typical charges and taxes are deducted:

Table 2: Annual returns from Irish asset classes (after taxes and charges)

	Cash	Bonds	Property	Equities	Inflation
30 yrs	8.0%	7.8%	n/a	12.3%	8.2%
25 yrs	8.5%	9.1%	9.7%	12.1%	8.4%
20 yrs	8.4%	9.1%	9.6%	13.0%	6.5%
15 yrs	7.4%	9.8%	6.6%	16.2%	3.8%
10 yrs	6.4%	8.0%	8.7%	12.9%	2.6%
5 yrs	5.0%	8.8%	10.3%	20.5%	2.0%

The table (above) describes the returns that would have been achieved by various asset classes assuming typical current charges of a 5% bid/offer spread and 1% management charge, and assuming the 24% standard rate of tax applied throughout.

So where's the catch?

As you can see from the returns in the table, investing in equities provided the best return in the past, in the long run. The price investors paid for this superior performance is 'volatility'. In other words, **while the result of investing in equities was better, the journey was a much bumpier one.**

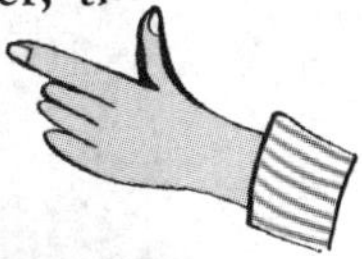

Table 3: Number of times markets fell (comparing year-end values) 1966-1997

	Bonds	*Property*	*Equities*
Over 1 year	7 times	Twice	13 times
Over 3 years	Once	None	4 times
Over 5 years	Once	None	Once
Over 10 years	None	None	None

Source: The Society of Actuaries in Ireland 1996/updated by BIAM 1998

That's the key difference between long-term and short-term saving. When you save, you know what you'll get and you know how long it will take to get there.

Experience shows that when you invest, you can expect to do much better in the long run, provided you are prepared to sit out the times when your investment drops in value, which it will from time to time.

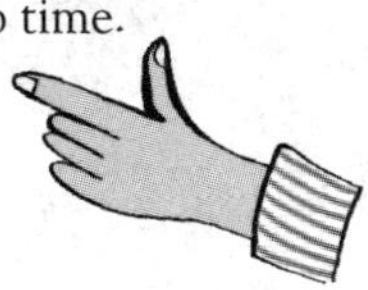

Part II

The Basics

The next five chapters cover the major asset classes in more detail. While it is designed as a beginners' guide – more seasoned investors may also find this section of use.

inflation
investments
deposits
deposits
investments

Chapter 3

'Inflation-proofing' your wealth

Inflation is always a threat to savings and investments. Put simply, inflation is the rate at which your money loses its ability to buy things.

Since 1966, inflation in Ireland has averaged 8.2 per cent per year. In the worst year (1975), inflation reached the dizzy heights of 20.9 per cent. Although inflation has been much lower in recent years (an average of 2.44 per cent per year in the nineties), it serves to remind us of just how high inflation can be.

Inflation can do considerable damage. If £1 was left lying under the mattress in 1966, it would be worth 8.7p today.

Even if inflation was at the (historically low) level of just 3% a year, your income and wealth would lose over a quarter of its value every ten years.

Keeping inflation at bay

If your money is on deposit, the interest earned is the first line of defence against inflation. At present, with interest rates at historically low levels, after-tax deposit rates are, once again, barely ahead of inflation.

In the last thirty years, inflation was higher than the after-tax rate of interest nearly once every two years. This mostly occurred from 1969 to 1983. Since the mid-eighties net interest rates have been ahead of inflation. Nonetheless, this piece of financial history serves to warn us of the need to do more long-term inflation-proofing of our wealth.

The most effective way to provide protection against inflation is to put at least part of your capital in assets that have substantially outperformed inflation in the long run. That usually means equities and property.

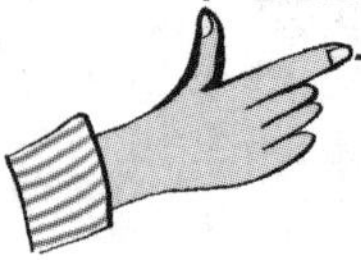

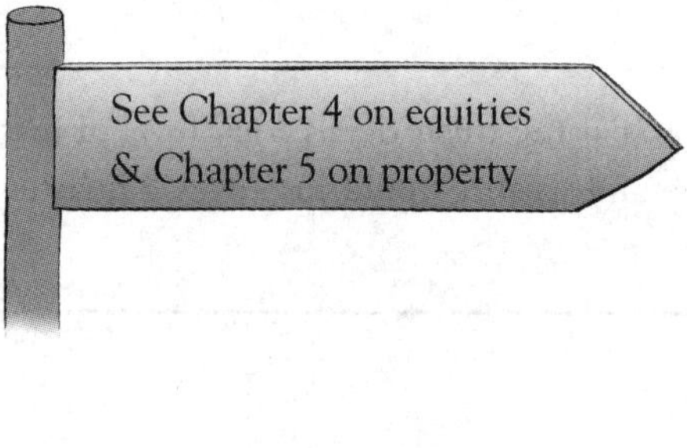

TABLE 1: THE LONG-TERM RETURNS TABLE

Annual returns from Irish asset classes (before taxes and charges) 1966 to 1997

	Cash	*Bonds*	*Property*	*Equities*	*Inflation*
30 yrs	10.5%	11.6%	n/a	16.7%	8.2%
25 yrs	11.1%	13.2%	14.2%	16.4%	8.4%
20 yrs	11.1%	13.4%	14.2%	18.2%	6.5%
15 yrs	9.8%	14.6%	10.4%	22.5%	3.8%
10 yrs	8.4%	12.4%	13.4%	18.3%	2.6%
5 yrs	6.6%	14.1%	16.3%	29.7%	2.0%

The table (above) describes the returns achieved by various asset classes from 1966 to 1997, as measured in a paper produced for The Society of Actuaries in Ireland in 1996, updated by BIAM in 1998. Returns do not reflect any charges or taxes which would reduce the returns.

A glance at the Long-Term Returns Table, which we introduced in Chapter 2, shows where the best long-term inflation-proofing is to be found. The answer is straightforward: deposits are best for short-term needs but, in the long term, equities and property are the asset classes that are most capable of delivering 'inflation-proof' returns.

Shares

Chapter 4

Investing in company shares

When you buy a share, you become part owner of a business and your investment participates in the success or failure of that business.

The reward for owning a share comes either in the income the company pays in annual dividends or in the growth in the share price. The better people think the company will do, the more growth you'll see in the share price.

On the other hand, industry and commerce always involve risk. Even when an economy is growing rapidly, some companies can still run into trouble. Although most quality shares do well in the long run, there is always the possibility of making a loss.

The big advantage of shares

> Historically, high quality shares have, on average, tended to do better than any other class of investment, beating property, bonds, and deposits. Let's take another look at the Long-Term Returns Table.

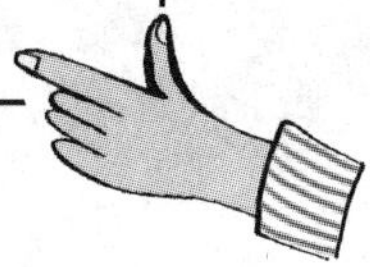

TABLE 1: THE LONG-TERM RETURNS TABLE

Annual returns from Irish asset classes (before taxes and charges) 1966 to 1997

	Cash	*Bonds*	*Property*	*Equities*	*Inflation*
30 yrs	10.5%	11.6%	n/a	16.7%	8.2%
25 yrs	11.1%	13.2%	14.2%	16.4%	8.4%
20 yrs	11.1%	13.4%	14.2%	18.2%	6.5%
15 yrs	9.8%	14.6%	10.4%	22.5%	3.8%
10 yrs	8.4%	12.4%	13.4%	18.3%	2.6%
5 yrs	6.6%	14.1%	16.3%	29.7%	2.0%

The table (above) describes the returns achieved by various asset classes from 1966 to 1997, as measured in a paper produced for The Society of Actuaries in Ireland in 1996, updated by BIAM in 1998. Returns do not reflect any charges or taxes which would reduce the returns.

Why does this happen?

The answer to this question lies at the heart of our economic system. Businesses have to earn more than they owe to stay in business. Our economy rewards those who create wealth, employment and prosperity for the rest of society. If it failed to reward the effort that this takes, then everybody would invest for secure returns and there would be less new wealth created in the country.

Equities: Investment characteristics

Growth 

Access 

Security 

So what's the catch?

Despite the 'growing power' of the stock market, it carries with it the risk of any business. There are good times and bad times and these are reflected in stock prices.

If you could transport yourself back to the stock market crash of 1987, things would have looked pretty bleak.

An investment worth £10,000 in an Irish equity fund on Friday 16 October 1987 would have been worth just £8,279 by the following Friday. What could the investor have done in these circumstances? Let's look at three possible options:-

- Cut one's losses and put the £8,279 on deposit. By April 1998 this would be worth £11,577.
- Stay put and wait for the recovery. By April 1998, this would be worth £26,311.
- Seize the buying opportunity. If the investor left the investment to recover and added a further £10,000, the total investment would now be worth £57,244.

Note: The equity returns are based on the performance of the average Irish equity fund, as defined by Moneymate, over the period shown, on an offer to bid basis. The deposit example given is based on a typical share deposit account, in this case the First National Investment Share Account. Figures supplied by Moneymate. Figures were estimated to 3 April 1998.

History of stock markets ... more of the same.

If you look back over the past twenty years, there are plenty of examples of the stock market's ability to disappoint in the short term…

…and of its ability to bounce back in relatively short periods of time!

Table 4: Lessons from stock market history

What goes down...	**...tends to go back up**
1929 to 1931 Worldwide economic recession saw 45% wiped off the value of equities.	*From 1931 to 1936* The value of shares nearly doubled in real terms
1970 to 1974 Equities in the UK fell 65% in real terms following the oil crisis.	*From Christmas 1974 to January 1975* Stock markets had risen 65%. By the beginning of 1976 the market was back where it was before the oil crisis.
19th October 1987 Share prices collapsed with a 23% drop in value in just one day. (Dow Jones Index).	*By December 1987* Share values had recovered to their January 1987 levels in real terms.

Readers should note that past performance of any of the investments mentioned in this book is not an indication of future performance, which will depend on future economic conditions.

There are words used by the investment industry that are unfamiliar to the ordinary investor. Here's an explanation of a few of the terms that will help when it comes to reading the financial pages.

Table 5: Understanding the lingo

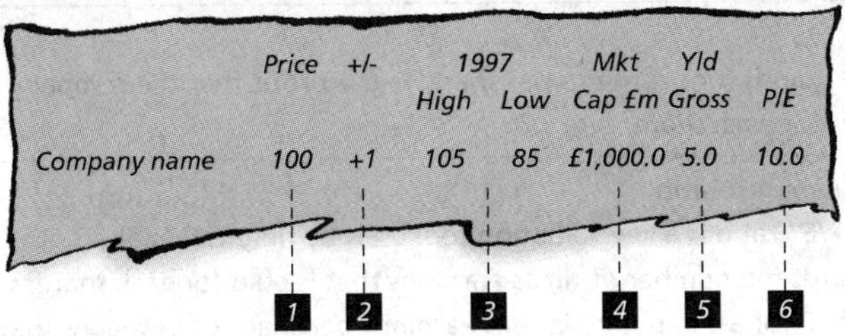

1 Share price: Usually this is expressed in pence unless otherwise stated.

2 Change in price: The change in price from the previous day.

3 The highest and lowest price achieved by the share over the previous twelve months.

4 Market capitalisation is equal to the value of all common shares in issue multiplied by the current share price, in other words, the value of the company.

5 The yield is the annual dividend as a % of the share price.

6 P/E ratio – the Price/Earnings ratio calculated by dividing the price of a share by the earnings per share.

Table 6: Key words to get to know
Share price The price at which the share trades on the stock exchange.
Dividend The amount the company pays out of its earnings as an annual income to investors. It is usually paid in two instalments.
EPS "EPS" stands for "earnings per share" – the profit that the company makes for each share.
Price-earnings ratio The "P/E" ratio is a key valuation tool used by financial analysts. It measures the number of times earnings that is paid for each share: so a P/E of 12 for a company that has earnings per share of £1 means that you have to pay £12 to acquire £1 of earnings generated by that company. The higher a P/E is the more expensive and/or more highly valued the share is.
Capitalisation The value of the company, given by the number of shares multiplied by the price of each share.
Dividend yield The dividend yield is calculated by dividing the dividend paid on each share by the share price.
Blue chip These are shares that are generally considered to be the most solid and reliable in the market.

Chapter 5

Investing in property

Irish investors are no strangers to the excellent returns that the property market has delivered in recent years. In the long term (twenty years or more), the performance of property compares well with other types of investment. Historically, commercial property has tended to beat cash but fall short of the performance of equities.

In addition, property investors have benefited from numerous tax advantages, which have added to and supplemented the returns. The short-term performance of property does not always coincide with that of the other major types of investment, such as company shares, so property can at times be a very useful way to diversify your investments.

In addition, property returns have tended to be less volatile than equities.

Property: Investment characteristics

Growth 

Access 

Security 

When comparing the returns of property investments to those achieved by equity investments, investors should always bear in mind that property returns also come with other advantages, especially tax benefits, greater predictability and higher income (rental), typically.

TABLE 1: LONG-TERM RETURNS TABLE

Annual returns from Irish asset classes (before taxes and charges) 1966 to 1997

	Cash	*Bonds*	*Property*	*Equities*	*Inflation*
30 yrs	10.5%	11.6%	n/a	16.7%	8.2%
25 yrs	11.1%	13.2%	14.2%	16.4%	8.4%
20 yrs	11.1%	13.4%	14.2%	18.2%	6.5%
15 yrs	9.8%	14.6%	10.4%	22.5%	3.8%
10 yrs	8.4%	12.4%	13.4%	18.3%	2.6%
5 yrs	6.6%	14.1%	16.3%	29.7%	2.0%

The table (above) describes the returns achieved by various asset classes from 1966 to 1997, as measured in a paper produced for The Society of Actuaries in Ireland in 1996, updated by BIAM in 1998. Returns do not reflect any charges or taxes which would reduce the returns.

Property performance and equity performance can also be compared by analysing pooled funds that specialise in each asset.

IR£10,000 invested in the average property fund on 1 January 1980 would have grown to IR£33,752 by April 1998. The average equity fund would have grown to IR£110,967 over the same period.

Figure 2: Property funds v equity funds
Value of IR£10,000 invested in 1980

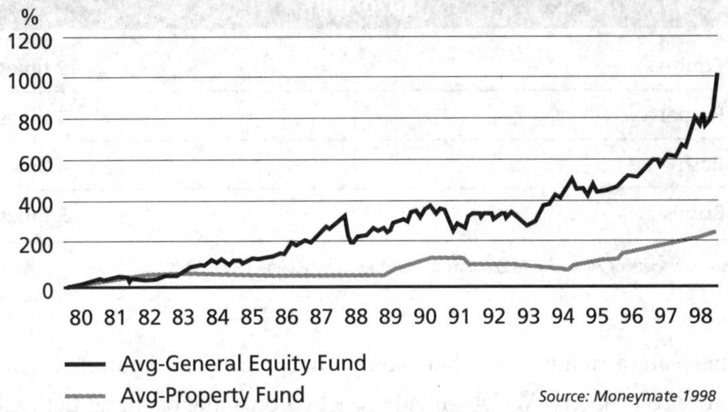

Source: Moneymate 1998

Note: Estimates are based on the average fund as defined by Moneymate and are measured from 1 January 1980 to 3 April 1998 on an offer to bid basis. Past performance is not an indication of future performance which will depend on future economic conditions.

Despite not performing as well as equities in the long run, property is a steadier performer. In fact, over the period 1970 to 1997, property was the top performer for Irish investors in no less than nine years – most often in the years when equities disappointed. This performance, when added to the resilience of property compared to the disappointments that stock markets sometimes deliver, goes a long way to explaining why so many Irish investors prefer the 'bricks and mortar' approach.

Table 7: Best-performing Irish asset class calendar years, 1970-1997

Equities	12 times
Property	9 times
Cash	4 times
Bonds	3 times

Source: Society of Actuaries in Ireland, 1996/updated by BIAM 1998

There are a number of other factors that need consideration when it comes to property. We've already touched on some of these. Let's take a brief look at each.

Borrowing

It is worth remembering that property is probably the easiest of investments to 'gear up'. This means it is usually easier to borrow from a lending institution when a property is being used as collateral, even if that property is to be used to generate rental income.

In general, most lenders will provide 'residential for letting' mortgages at a premium to the standard domestic mortgage – often at one to two per cent higher interest rates. Most lenders will not lend as high a percentage of the purchase price as they would with domestic properties (although this varies from lender to lender). With low interest rates, rental income can often match interest payments on borrowings, leaving capital appreciation to the investor.

The terms that lenders offer for commercial mortgages for industrial or commercial properties are usually packaged for the individual property.

Tax and incentives

A wide variety of tax incentives exist for the investor who is considering property investment. These include:

Capital allowances – industrial buildings

An individual who invests in a qualifying industrial building can avail of capital allowances that may reduce their tax bill. The maximum an individual can claim following the 1998 budget is IR£25,000 per year.

Capital allowances – residential property

It is possible to avail of capital allowances if an individual invests in a residential property. The level of allowance that can be claimed will depend on the type of property and its location.

Capital allowances – other

A variety of capital allowances are available for investments made in the following:

- enterprise areas
- hotels
- resorts
- shops
- offices
- private nursing homes

Once again, the level of the allowance and its use as an offset against non-rental income will depend on the type and location of the investment.

Costs and liquidity

The positive features that come with tax incentives and borrowing have to be offset against the costs and time involved in investing in property and the illiquidity associated with this type of investment.

Property needs to be managed and maintained – which can be costly (although certain expenses can be offset against income for tax purposes). This is generally not the case with other asset classes. In addition, if you wish to cash in your investment, it can take a great deal more time than other investments. Transaction costs will generally be considerably higher for property than for other investments. Stamp duty and legal costs are the most obvious examples of the types of transaction costs involved.

Summary

To summarise, property has tended not to perform as well as the stock market in the long run; but a variety of tax advantages (and the country's instinctive preference for 'the land') maintains its popularity as an investment.

Chapter 6

Investing in bonds

Ever wonder how the government borrows money? Or big companies, for that matter? The method they often use is the issuing of 'bonds'.

When a bond is issued the investor is lending money to the government or to a company. In return, the government or company generally guarantees to pay a fixed amount of interest and to repay the original amount after a pre-arranged period.

Once bonds are issued, most can then be bought and sold on the stock exchange – just like shares. Despite the fact that bonds like these usually pay a fixed amount of interest, the price of the bond will move up and down. It's not the rate of interest on the bond that changes, it is its attractiveness compared with other investments. So, for example, if interest rates rise and a person can get a higher rate of interest, then the value of the bond with the lower interest rate will fall (and vice versa).

Bonds usually have the following features:

- name – simply to help investors identify it!
- nominal value that the issuer promises to repay at an agreed date in the future
- fixed income paid out each year, stated as a percentage of the nominal value; this is known in the industry as the 'coupon'
- redemption or repayment date
- a market price – which will change all the time

Are these investments risk-free?

Historically, bonds have tended to be less risky investments than shares. However, that is not to say that they don't have risks of their own.

There is always a risk (however small) that the issuer will default on the bond. There is also some risk that the demand for a certain bond may fall. More importantly, however, because bonds trade on the stock exchange and their price will vary, there is a risk of the return being less than expected if the bond is sold before maturity. The biggest factor affecting the price and, therefore, the return is the prevailing/expected rate of interest.

Bonds: Investment characteristics

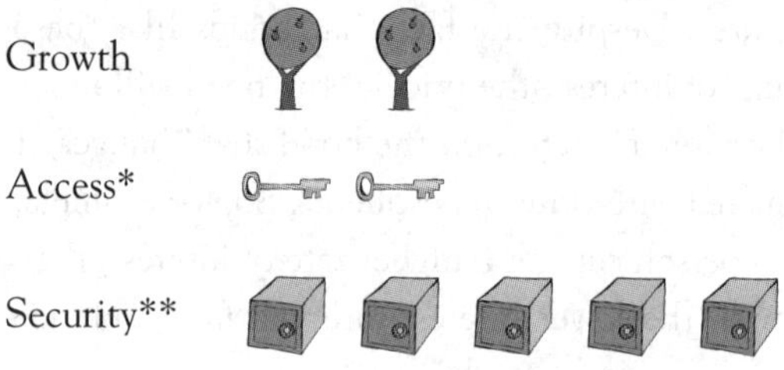

**Access may be much greater than indicated, but at the cost of reduced capital security.*
***Security may vary depending on the creditworthiness of the issuer of the bond.*

So how well have government bonds done in the past?

Government bonds are often considered to be a less volatile and safer investment than shares. In general, this has been so in the past. This greater security has always come at a price. If you look back over the past three decades, bonds have provided a steady performance over inflation.

TABLE 1: THE LONG-TERM RETURNS TABLE

Annual returns from Irish asset classes (before taxes and charges) 1966 to 1997

	Cash	*Bonds*	*Property*	*Equities*	*Inflation*
30 yrs	10.5%	11.6%	n/a	16.7%	8.2%
25 yrs	11.1%	13.2%	14.2%	16.4%	8.4%
20 yrs	11.1%	13.4%	14.2%	18.2%	6.5%
15 yrs	9.8%	14.6%	10.4%	22.5%	3.8%
10 yrs	8.4%	12.4%	13.4%	18.3%	2.6%
5 yrs	6.6%	14.1%	16.3%	29.7%	2.0%

The table (above) describes the returns achieved by various asset classes from 1966 to 1997, as measured in a paper produced for The Society of Actuaries in Ireland in 1996, updated by BIAM in 1998. Returns do not reflect any charges or taxes which would reduce the returns.

Along the way, bond values would certainly have seen some ups and downs but nothing like the level of variation you would have seen in a share portfolio.

There was a drop in the value of Irish bonds in seven of the last thirty-two years, if you compared calendar year returns.

In contrast, you would have seen thirteen falls in value in Irish shares over the same period, if you compare year-end values.

Table 3: Number of times markets fell (comparing year-end values) 1966-1997

	Bonds	*Property*	*Equities*
Over 1 year	7 times	Twice	13 times
Over 3 years	Once	None	4 times
Over 5 years	Once	None	Once
Over 10 years	None	None	None

Source: The Society of Actuaries in Ireland 1996/updated by BIAM 1998

Where can I invest in a bond?

Although some people do invest directly in government bonds through stockbrokers, it is common to invest in bonds as part of a managed fund. They are usually part of the mix of investments that underlie these funds, as they are seen as a way to diversify funds away from some of the ups and downs of equities.

As with equities, bonds have many terms that ordinary investors do not encounter often. Here's an explanation that will help when reading the financial pages:

Table 8: Understanding the lingo

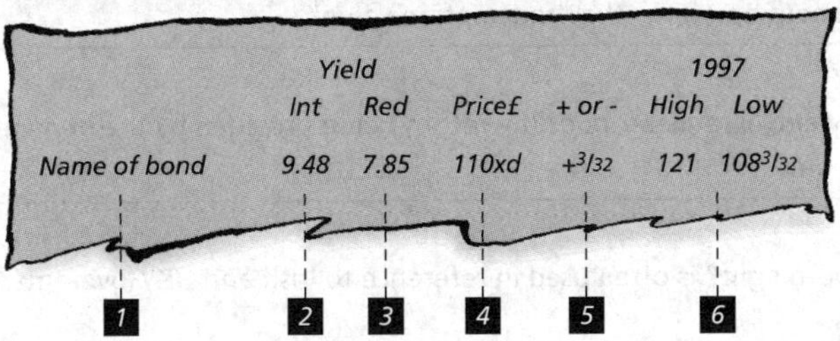

1. The name of the bond will typically be something like 9¾% Cap 1/6/98 – which means this bond will pay out £9.75 for every £100 of stock held. In 1998, the government will redeem the stock you hold.
2. This is the actual interest paid to an investor, expressed as a percentage of the current price.
3. The redemption yield is the average return you'll earn before tax if you hold the bond until maturity.
4. This is the current market price of the bond.
5. Change in price over the previous day's price.
6. This shows the highest and lowest price achieved by the bond over the previous twelve months.

Table 9: Understanding the lingo

Coupon

Bonds will pay a fixed rate of interest, usually every six months. This rate is known as the "coupon".

Redemption value

When the bond reaches maturity it usually repays the original investment amount – the "redemption value".

Yield

The "yield" is a measure of the return being provided by the bond at a given time.

Gilt

The word "gilt" is often used in reference to Irish and UK Government bonds.

Corporate bonds

Bonds issued by large companies are referred to as "corporate bonds". Conventional wisdom holds that corporate bonds provide a higher return for a higher risk.

Junk bond

High-risk corporate bonds.

Credit rating

Every bond issued is only as good as the issuer's word; so each one comes with a credit rating to help investors understand any risk involved.

Time to maturity

The amount of time left before the issuer has to pay back the amount invested.

Investment Advice on Life

Chapter 7

Investing for the faint-hearted

The heading is deliberate. The great majority of us are faint-hearted when it comes to investing. Many of us prefer to steer clear of the headline-grabbing booms and busts that seem to go hand in hand with stock markets and other high performing investments. Even armed with the knowledge that these investments do significantly better in the long run (despite the ups and downs), many people simply do not want to see any volatility in their nest egg's value.

> **Be warned, though. As we have already illustrated in earlier chapters, security and peace of mind have their own price – and that price is *usually* a reduced rate of return in the long run.**

Secure long-term savings

When it comes to long-term savings there are two things to consider:

- For how long are you prepared to lock away your money?
- With whom should you invest?

The longer you are prepared to leave your money invested, the better the return you can expect, in general.

With regard to long-term secure savings there are probably three to four main alternatives:

- Term deposits. It can be worth investigating long-term deposit rates – some banks offer deposits over one or two years that can be attractive, and there are deposits available that go out as far as five or six years.
- Guaranteed bonds, available from major life assurance companies (usually over three to six years in term). These offer a simple percentage return after an agreed number of years. Some versions offer income and a return of the original capital after a number of years.
- Savings Certificates (five years) and Savings Bonds (three years) from An Post. Again, these offer a simple straightforward percentage return. Returns from An Post can be attractive, but remember to compare with other secure investments.
- Secure, low risk managed funds (which are open-ended and easily accessible, although they usually carry entry charges). These funds generally invest either exclusively in cash or in both cash and bonds.

It is often well worthwhile spending time shopping around for the best interest rate. In more recent times, the rates available have dropped significantly and the difference between the best and the worst is no longer as dramatic. Nonetheless, it can be worth looking at a number of institutions.

Check the car!

When comparing interest rates, always be sure you're comparing like with like.

For example, 40% after five years is not the same as 8% per year over five years. Why not? Compound interest! We can see the affect this has with a simple example:

Table 10: Comparing interest rates; IR£10,000 example

Year	*40% after 5 years*	*8% per year*
1	–	£10,800
2	–	£11,664
3	–	£12,597
4	–	£13,605
5	£14,000	£14,693

A worthwhile tip is to compare the 'C.A.R.' that is quoted with nearly all the returns indicated. C.A.R. stands for 'compound annual return', and it's the best way of comparing what's really on offer. In our example, the 'C.A.R.' for 40% over five years is 6.96% per year. Not all institutions are obliged to publish it, so be sure to ask.

Secure long-term investments

Tracker bonds have been popular long-term secure investments in recent years.

They are available from most banks, building societies, life assurance companies and certain stockbrokers.

These investments offer a less risky way to get access to returns related to the stock market. These investments offer 'bottom-line' security – so if stock markets fail to perform over a selected number of years, the original investment is generally returned. In addition, the bond gives a return that is based on the growth in a stock market index or basket of indices.

They offer the potential to make better returns than the more secure deposit based savings plans. In common with long-term savings plans, you have to lock your money away for a number of years. However, with trackers there is an element of risk that the chosen stock markets will not deliver over the period selected.

In most cases, diversifying across a number of markets and opting for the longer term (five years or more) should give the bond time to deliver better returns.

Key things to look out for:

- in general, stock market related investing is best done over five years or more
- try to get a wide basket of quality stock markets if you are not an experienced investor.

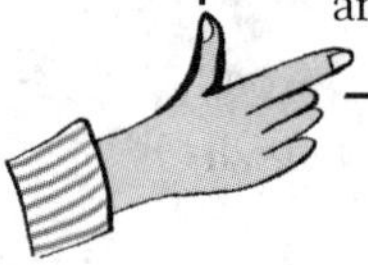

Lower risk pooled funds

In addition to tracker bonds, most fund management houses and life assurers offer ranges of less risky unit-linked funds and unit trusts. These funds typically invest mostly in cash and bonds, with a smaller proportion invested in equities than the typical managed fund.

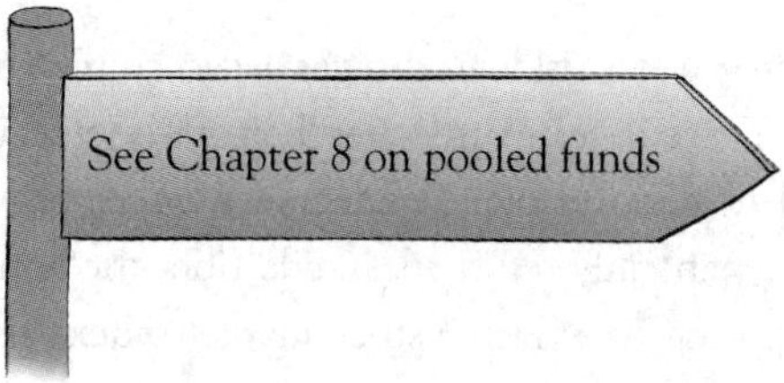

Part III

More about Investing

In Part III we discuss a broad range of investment products, what they provide and what investors should look for.

Chapter 8

A dip into pooled investments

Investing directly

Many people invest by buying shares or property directly from stockbrokers, estate agents and other property companies. There are advantages to this approach, such as:

- the choice of which individual shares or property to invest in
- individual tax advantages especially with property investments
- the ability to use your personal capital gains tax allowance and to offset losses
- a lower level of transaction costs if you are only holding a small number of assets.

Investing directly means incurring transaction charges and handling all the tax requirements yourself. For the smaller investor, this can be a disincentive.

Pooled investments

'Pooled investments' are an alternative that can reduce both the cost of investing and the paperwork involved.

In simple terms, a group of investors pool their money to gain the benefits of being a single, large investor. This enables them to invest in a wider range of investments and to employ a professional investment manager to manage their money. The majority of pooled investments invest in company shares and government bonds. Some also invest in property and cash type investments.

There are three broad categories of pooled investments that are available in Ireland:

- Unit trusts/unit-linked funds
- With-profit bonds
- Tracker bonds

Unit trusts & unit-linked funds

Unit trusts

Unit trusts are probably the simplest way of investing in stock markets and involve a group of investors, a fund manager who manages the investments and a trustee who supervises the fund manager and makes sure that the job is done properly.

Unit-linked funds

A unit-linked fund is very similar to a unit trust. The difference is that the unit-linked fund has a life assurance policy attached to it and does not have trustees.

How do they differ?

For most investors, there is no significant difference between unit trusts and unit-linked funds. Both are pooled investments that are now taxed similarly, although this was not the case historically.

Most unit trusts and unit-linked funds provide a wide range of options from which investors can choose.

When you invest in a unit trust or unit-linked fund, your money buys a certain number of units. The value of these units goes up and down as the value of the underlying assets change.

The choice of unit trusts and unit-linked funds is very wide, so there is something for everyone. Generally, however, they fall into one of three categories:

Secure funds (low risk)
which invest in very secure, generally short-term investments, to provide steady capital growth.

Balanced funds (medium risk)
which invest in a wide range of assets, both at home and overseas, with a view to providing enhanced capital growth.

Specialist funds (higher risk)
which invest in a specific asset, such as company shares or property, or a specific region, such as the UK, Ireland, or the US, with the objective of providing superior long-term growth.

With-profit bonds

These have been available for many years and are offered by a number of life assurance companies.

With-profit bonds invest in the same type of assets as other pooled investments. The value of underlying assets can go up and down in just the same way as other pooled investments.

However, With-profit bonds differ in a number of ways:

- You have to decide in advance how long you want to invest for – often 10 years or more.
- With-profit bonds are designed to 'smooth out' returns. The life assurance company does this by providing the return to policyholders in three parts at the end of the specified term:
    - The 'guaranteed sum assured' is the minimum amount that is payable at the end of the term
    - Each year the assurance company adds a bonus to the guarantee (the 'reversionary bonus'), which is payable at the end of the term, generally.

- At the end of the term, the assurance company adds a further, usually larger, bonus (the 'terminal' bonus).

With-profit bonds are popular because they give a degree of security combined with good long-term prospects.

Generally, early encashment is not advisable, as much of the return comes with the final bonus, and there can be significant 'surrender penalties'. Also, investors should be aware that With-profit bonds usually contain a 'market value adjustment'. This clause entitles the company to reduce the final payout in the event of a major change in market conditions or if large numbers of investors look for their money at the same time.

Tracker bonds

Tracker bonds are usually set up as either deposits or life assurance policies (deposit versions are not pooled investments in the strictest sense). Trackers are available from most banks, building societies, life assurance companies and certain stockbrokers.

- The investment will typically last for a period of five or six years (although there are shorter terms available).
- In general, trackers provide capital security at the end of the selected term. Some also provide a secure return at the end of the term.
- Trackers provide a return based on the growth in a stock market index or basket of stock market indices. The most common indices used include FT-SE 100 (UK), S&P 500 (USA), Nikkei 300 (Japan), DAX (Germany), AEX (Holland), SMI (Switzerland), and CAC 40 (France). Other indices are also used.

- Remember, tracker bonds will provide a return that is limited to a market index or indices over a set number of years. They do not provide any dividends, which would accrue to a direct or pooled investment.

Trackers have become popular because they combine capital security with stock market related returns.

Before you invest, scrutinise the terms of a tracker bond carefully. Be sure you understand the following:

- **Limits**
  Some tracker bonds are restricted in the performance they can provide.
- **Quality markets**
  If you are not an experienced investor make sure you are investing in a wide selection of quality stock markets.
- **Averaging**
  Most trackers protect their gains against last minute volatility by giving a final return that is based on the average of the final months. Too short a period may not give enough protection but too long may restrict the returns.

Tax Treatments
* GROSS
* Exempt
* Net (standard rate)
* Net (special rate)

Chapter 9

Taxes and your investments

"I believe we should all pay taxes with a smile. I tried – but they wanted cash" – Anon

When choosing a home for your investment, you need to take account of the tax implications of your investment decision. However, tax is only one thing which should influence your investment decision. It should rarely, if ever, be the sole reason for choosing an investment.

Tax treatments

From a tax perspective, the return you get on an investment generally ends up in one of four broad categories;

- **Gross**
  Here, you have to take care of any or all tax liabilities yourself. This usually means either Capital Gains Tax or Income Tax.

- **Exempt**
  Returns from the investment are exempt from tax. In general, this type of return is restricted to pension funds and charities.

- **Net (standard rate)**
  The tax liability is paid for you by the investment and you have no further liability on the gains made.

- **Net (special rate)**
  The tax liability is deducted within the investment at a specially-reduced rate. Restrictions apply to where and how much can be invested.

Taking each of these categories in turn, the following is a broad outline of the types of liabilities that can result. Remember, when it comes to tax matters, these are broad generalisations. You should always check out your own individual circumstances before investing.

Gross investments

The list of investments that can result in you having to take care of a tax liability is extensive. In terms of long-term financial investments, however, the most common include direct holdings of stocks and shares, bonds and property. Most holdings of this nature result in Capital Gains Tax and/or Income Tax in some form.

Following the recent budget, a person is entitled to a Capital Gains Tax allowance of IR£1,000, with any gains beyond this being subject to tax at 20%. (Remember, indexation relief is still available)

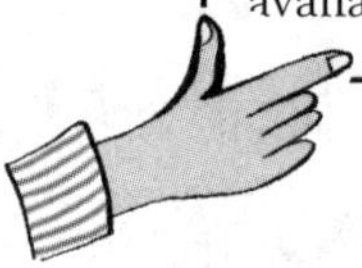

Exempt

Exempt investments include pensions and charity funds primarily. Both are generally allowed to grow free of tax. As an eligible individual you can invest up to 15% of your income (net relevant earnings) in a pension plan every year with full tax relief. In addition, the returns grow tax free, making it the most tax efficient way to invest.

Of course, you can't get at the proceeds until you retire so you'll have to be prepared for the long run.

Once you come to retire you can usually take up to a quarter of the fund as a tax-free lump sum. If you haven't got a pension already, our advice is to start one as early as you possibly can. If you are self-employed or in a company that does not provide pension facilities, you are eligible for a personal pension. Personal pensions are available through banks and from all of the country's life assurance companies.

One other way to invest your money that is completely tax-free is to place money with An Post (in their Savings Certificates and Savings Bonds). As secure products, these do not offer as much potential as some of the less secure investments. While An Post's returns can be very competitive, it is often worth looking at the taxable secure products offered by banks and life assurance companies and comparing returns.

Net (standard rate)

Most investments, such as managed funds, tracker bonds, unit trusts and all ordinary deposits are subject to tax at the standard rates. The tax, generally, is deducted and paid before you receive your return. In general, this rate applies irrespective of the income bracket in which you are.

Net (special rate)

Under the Finance Act, 1993 a new category of savings and investment products were introduced into Ireland. Special Savings Accounts (SSAs) are probably the best known of these. A Special Savings Account is a deposit account where an individual can save up to IR£50,000, with interest taxed at 20%. There are three other broad categories of 'special investments' covered under the legislation:-

i) Special Investment Schemes

ii) Special Investment Policies

iii) Special Portfolio Investment Accounts.

Special Investment Schemes are unit trusts managed by fund managers. Special Investment Policies are life assurance plans available from certain life assurance companies. Both are funds in which investors' returns are taxed at 10% as opposed to the normal 24%. To qualify for this reduced rate of tax, the fund has to invest at least 55% of its assets in Irish equities. Special Portfolio Investment Accounts are another variation that enable investors to select the stocks in which they are investing, within the 10% tax environment. An individual can invest up to IR£75,000 in a Special Investment depending on the amount held in a Special Savings Account. In general, the following limits apply to special investments for an individual:

When investing, given the amount of tax many of us pay already,

Table 11: Special investment limits

Amount in SSA	Limit in Special Investment
0	IR£75,000
0 – IR£25,000	IR£50,000
IR£25,000 – IR£50,000	IR£25,000

Note: Bases and rates of tax indicated are subject to change.

investors should always ensure they make optimum use of any tax advantages available with their preferred investment.

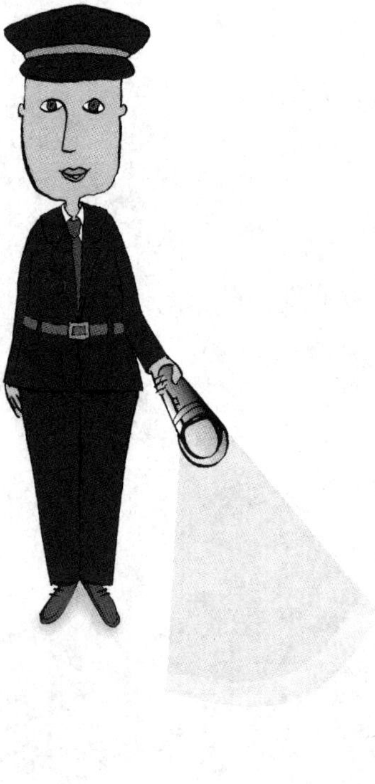

Chapter 10

Keeping the financial services industry in line

There are risks that you should not have to face as an investor – including receiving misleading advice, dealing with unauthorised persons, misappropriation of funds, and other activities that could lead you to invest in a way that you wouldn't otherwise do, or worse, could lead to losses that are beyond tolerable levels.

If problems do arise, the best advice is to present the problem to the financial institution with whom you are dealing. In the event that this fails to satisfy you, then, depending on the type of institution you are dealing with, there is a regulatory body to which you can turn.

> At the end of the day, the best advice for any investor is to take the following simple steps to ensure that their funds are safely invested.

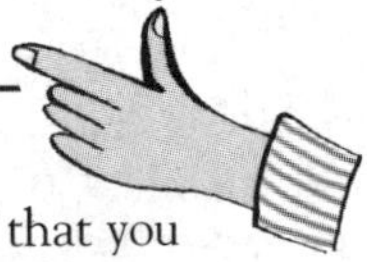

#1 With any financial transaction, make sure you have proof that you placed the money with the institution or intermediary. (This might be a receipt or a deposit book).

#2 If you are in doubt about the credentials of the person you are investing with, don't part with your money.

#3 If you are unclear about what the person is authorised to do, ask. Some financial intermediaries are not authorised to take deposits on behalf of deposit institutions. Others are not authorised to conduct investment business. Others may not be authorised to act as credit intermediaries for mortgages, finance, or leasing.

#4 Remember that if you are presented with an investment that appears 'too good to be true', it probably is. This is usually most apparent with investments that offer 'guaranteed' returns. With such products, investigate what the competition is offering; if there's a huge difference, ask why and be prepared to be sceptical about the answers you are given.

Who regulates Irish financial services?

Institution/ intermediary	*Who regulates?*
Banks, Building Societies, Investment managers and Intermediaries, Stockbrokers, other credit institutions	Central Bank of Ireland Dame Street, Dublin 2 Ombudsman for Credit Institutions 8 Adelaide Court Adelaide Road, Dublin 2 Director of Consumer Affairs, 4 Harcourt Road, Dublin 4
Pensions	Pensions Board Holbrook House, Holles Street, Dublin 2
Insurance	Irish Insurance Federation 39 Molesworth Street, Dublin 2 Department of Enterprise and Employment Kildare Street, Dublin 2 Office of the Insurance Ombudsman 39 Molesworth Street, Dublin 2
Insurance brokers	Irish Brokers Association 87 Merrion Square, Dublin 2 Irish Insurance Compliance Bureau 39 Molesworth Street, Dublin 2
Credit unions	Registrar of Friendly Societies Dublin Castle, Dublin 2
Credit intermediaries	Director of Consumer Affairs 4 Harcourt Road, Dublin 2

Part IV

More about the Stock Market

The stock market has an important role to play for long-term investors, so we've devoted three extra chapters to give experienced investors more information about this type of investment.

John
David
Mary

Chapter 11

What's in a name?

Some of the most spectacular returns in stock market history have come from some of the best-known brands in the world. If we look at three household brands, we'll get a sense of how extraordinary these stories are:

Coca-Cola

The world's biggest brand delivered spectacular returns to early investors, if they stayed around long enough to enjoy it. $10 invested in Coca-Cola shares in 1919 would now be worth a staggering $1,382,420 if all income had been reinvested. One investment commentator has noted: 'Several times a year, a weighty and serious investor looks long and with profound respect at Coca-Cola's record but comes regretfully to the conclusion that he is looking too late.' That was in 1938.

Gillette

The comfort in being an investor in Gillette comes from the fact that there are 2.5 billion men whose hair grows while they sleep! It has been estimated that 20 to 21 billion razor blades are used in the world each year. 30 per cent of these are made by Gillette, but they make up 60 per cent of the market in value terms.

Investors who bought $1,000 of Gillette shares back in 1950 would now be sitting on an investment worth an estimated $191,826.

Microsoft

More recently, the software giant Microsoft would have delivered some very impressive returns to investors. $10,000 invested in Microsoft back in 1986 would now be worth an estimated $1,853,125 if all income had been reinvested.

These worldwide market-leading companies possess some rare qualities. Warren Buffet, the legendary American investor, swears by them.

He is quoted as saying about Coca-Cola; 'Let's say you were going away for ten years and you wanted to make one investment decision, … and you couldn't change it while you're gone … If I came up with anything in terms of certainty … where I knew the leader was going to continue to be the leader … I just don't know anything like Coke.'

A British study on the performance of companies with strong brands such as Unilever, Cadburys and British Airways showed they had all done better than the UK market in general over the last fifteen years (as measured against the FT-SE 350 index). There are many reasons why this may be so: for example, branded products can command higher prices and can usually sell their product more easily into new countries.

Table 12: Coca-Cola consumption worldwide (cans per person per year)

USA	343
China	8
Indonesia	6
India	3

Source: Coca-Cola

As wealth in developing countries grows, the likelihood is that the big worldwide brands will find it easier to grow in these countries.

An example of this is the personal hygiene market in China.

Table 13: Market share of Chinese urban market

Toothpaste	
Crest	56 per cent
Toilet Soap	
Lux and Dove	78 per cent
Shampoo	
Pantene and Head & Shoulders	90 per cent

Source: Credit Lyonnais Asia

Despite charging a premium price compared with local alternatives, these western brands have already successfully penetrated China's cities and towns.

So, how can you invest in these brands?

There are two main routes: either buy the shares directly through a stockbroker, or invest in certain pooled funds. Both approaches have their advantages. By buying stocks directly, you can choose where you invest. If you invest in a pooled fund, a professional fund manager will often include leading brands in the selection of stocks in the fund (this will vary depending on the type of fund). The fund manager will make these selections and will take care of research and administration for you.

Remember, past performance is no guarantee of future returns

Chapter 12

'I'm afraid to invest, the market's too high.'

Should I try to 'time' my investment in the stock market?

If we compare the investors who got in at some of the best times with those who invested at some of the worst times we can get a clear sense of the difference this makes in the long run.

Best case: January 1974 to January 1998

The first example is that of a person who invested at some of the 'best times' over the past twenty-five years. Let's say this person invested IR£10,000 on six occasions that, in retrospect, seem well timed. Total investment: IR£60,000.

Figure 3: The world stock market 1974 to 1998 – better times to invest

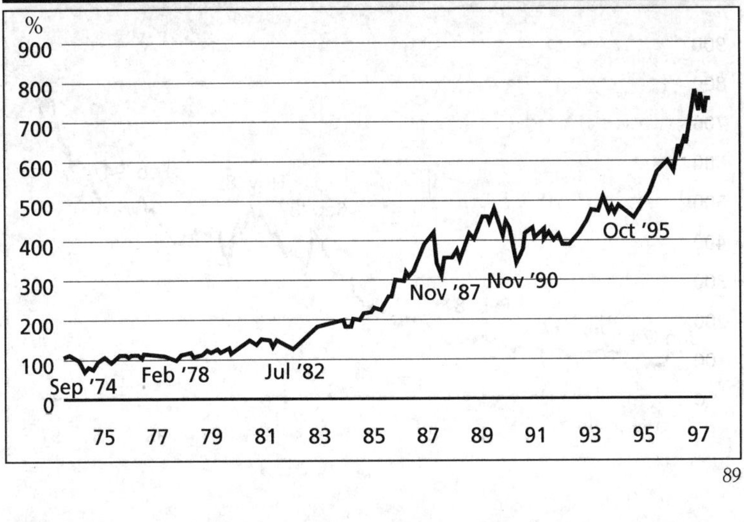

Table 14: Best case; 1970-1998

Date	*Amount*	*Value Jan '98*
Sep '74	IR£10,000	IR£475,698
Feb '78	IR£10,000	IR£244,764
July '82	IR£10,000	IR£118,194
Nov '87	IR£10,000	IR£36,473
Nov '90	IR£10,000	IR£32,292
Oct '95	IR£10,000	IR£17,140
TOTAL	IR£60,000	IR£924,561

The figures shown are based on the growth in the MSCI World Index including reinvestment of dividends. This does not include charges or taxes that might have applied. Past performance is not an indication of future performance, which will depend on future economic conditions.

Worst case: January 1974 to January 1998

The second case is the investor who invests at times that, with hindsight, were not the best periods for investment in stock markets.

Figure 4: The world stock market 1974 to 1998 –worse times to invest

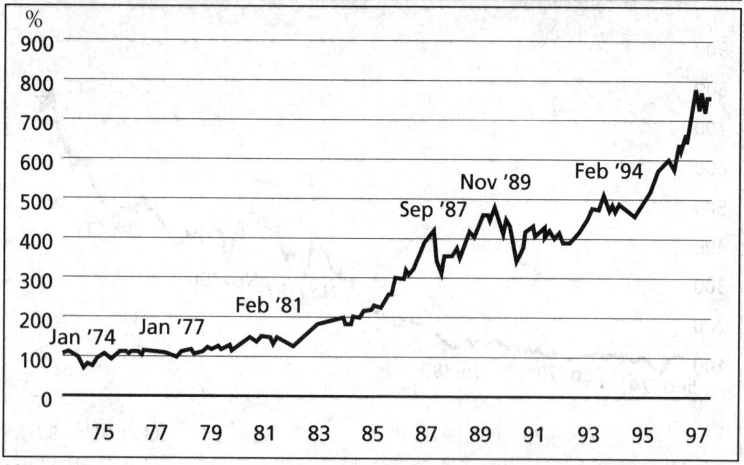

Table 15: Worst case; 1970-1998

Date	*Amount*	*Value Jan '98*
Jan '74	IR£10,000	IR£327,297
Jan '77	IR£10,000	IR£220,083
Feb '81	IR£10,000	IR£125,927
Sep '87	IR£10,000	IR£26,570
Nov '89	IR£10,000	IR£22,681
Feb '94	IR£10,000	IR£17,297
TOTAL	IR£60,000	IR£739,855

The figures shown are based on the growth in the MSCI World Index including reinvestment of dividends. This does not include charges or taxes that might have applied. Past performance is not an indication of future performance, which will depend on future economic conditions.

The difference between the two is by no means trivial! However, both portfolios had grown significantly in value – the best one by 15.4 times and the worst one by 12.3 times. Both would have been a long way ahead of the best deposit account over that period.

In reality, the great majority of investors would have bought at neither the cheapest nor the most expensive time every time they invested, so most people would be somewhere in the middle.

The most simple of all approaches to this problem is to completely ignore the ups and downs of the stock market and to pursue a plan of regular investment.

A strategy of investing regularly, irrespective of the state of the stock market, quite simply means you can be sure that part of your money invests at the 'best times', part at 'average times', and part at the 'worst times' – so you won't make the mistake of putting all your money into the market at the wrong time.

In the financial industry, this approach is called 'pound cost averaging'. Don't be put off by the elaborate-sounding name. Pound cost averaging can reduce, although not eliminate, the risk of equity market investment, by ensuring that you don't invest your entire portfolio at temporarily high prices. To get the benefit, you have to be tenacious and continue to invest during the bad times in the same way as during good times.

The stock market at IR£1.30 a day – PIPs & PEPs

For those who have no lump sum to start off with, there is a range of regular investment plans (known generally as 'PIPs' and 'PEPs') available from the country's banks and life assurance companies that, by their nature, use this approach to investment.

In recent times, the cost of these plans has come down dramatically and it is possible to start investing in these plans from as little as IR£40 to IR£50 a month (roughly IR£1.30 a day).

PIPs are regular investment plans that invest small amounts, usually monthly, in pooled funds, such as those we talked about in Chapter 8.

PEPs also invest in pooled funds but tend to specialise in investing more heavily in the Irish stock market and enjoy a 10% tax rate, compared to the 24% currently applying to PIPs.

As with all investments, these plans need time to deliver strong returns to investors – usually seven or more years is recommended.

The lesson for the more seasoned investor

Timing the stock market is a very difficult, some say impossible, thing to get right.

> The more reliable ingredient that investors should include in their investment mix is time, and as much of it as can be afforded.

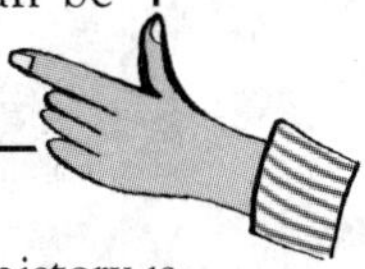

Time will not ensure that you get the maximum return but, if history is anything to go by, it will help to ensure that your investment provides very strong absolute returns.

Bonds
Stock's

Chapter 13

Bulls may be running but bears are lurking

The saying goes, 'Bull markets are born on pessimism, grow on scepticism, mature on optimism and die on euphoria'. Throughout the history of investments, markets are dotted with examples of the dreaded 'crash'. The more spectacular ones have lived long in the folklore of investments.

Table 16: Examples of major (& recent) stock market crashes in the 20th century

When	*What happened*
1929	**'Black Thursday' 1929** The US stock market lost 12.6 per cent in a single day, sending shock waves around world markets and sparking the 'Great Depression'. A total of 45 per cent was lost in real terms by 1931.
1974-75	**OPEC price rise** Inflation, oil price increases, and industrial unrest conspired to produce dramatic losses in stock markets. In March 1974, equities fell by 22 per cent. The bottom didn't come until December 1974.
1987	**'Black Monday' – 19 October 1987** The US market lost 22.6 per cent of its value in a single day, with similar losses in other major world markets.
1990	**Japanese stock market collapses** From its peak in 1990 the Japanese market has lost over 60 per cent of its value in the most prolonged bear market in a developed market in decades.
1997	**Hong Kong and the Far East** On 22 October 1997, the Hang Seng Index lost 10 per cent – its biggest one-day fall.

Dramatic crashes are, however, infrequent events. Stock markets generally go through slightly more gentle ups and downs than these dramatic events suggest.

Nonetheless, crashes can and do happen, and what's more, they tend to happen out of the blue. Although we'd all like to have some advance warning of coming collapses, this is simply not always possible. Despite this, abandoning the stock market is not necessarily the best approach. Investors who saw the effects of the biggest percentage drop in recent history in 1987, have since learnt the lesson that panic can be the most expensive of strategies.

What to do in case of a crash

In the case of stock market crashes, safety first may not always be the best approach. It's worth examining the last major crash in western markets (1987) to see what we mean.

We already looked at one possible set of scenarios following that crash in Chapter 4 and it's worth repeating it here. Consider the person who invested IR£10,000 in an Irish equity fund on Friday 16 October 1987. The market collapsed the following Monday and by the following Friday the investment would have been worth just IR£8,279.

The investor who saw disaster all around and opted for a safety first approach may have cashed in and put the IR£8,279 on deposit. By April 1998 this would have been worth IR£11,577. If the fund remained invested it would have faced further losses. By December 1987, it would have been valued at just IR£5,887, a loss of 41 per cent in less than two months. The fund began recovering from then and by April 1989 had regained its original value. By April 1998 the fund would have been worth IR£26,311.

If a further IR£10,000 was added to the fund the week after the crash, the total investment would have been worth IR£57,244 by April 1998.

Note: The equity returns are based on the performance of the average Irish equity fund over the period indicated on an offer to bid basis. The deposit example given is based on a typical share deposit account, in this case the First National Investment Share Account. Figures supplied by Moneymate. Past performance is not an indication of future performance, which will depend on future economic conditions.

Another lesson to learn from the recent past is that most 'crashes' tend not to be prolonged and, while there are exceptions, they are infrequent (the Japanese market is the most obvious example of a market that has been a long time waiting for a recovery).

If the economic fundamentals are sound (i.e. a stable economy with low interest rates and low inflation), then recovery is usually relatively fast. Usually, it is only when there are substantial economic difficulties that recovery in markets can take longer. Prolonged bear markets, however, can and do happen. One notable period was the early seventies following the oil price crisis. The jump in oil prices, soaring inflation and unprecedented industrial unrest conspired to produce a very prolonged bear market. During March 1974 the UK stock market lost 22 per cent. Having recovered slightly by May, it then faced the worst seven months in London stock market history, halving in value. If the crash was dramatic, then the recovery was even more so – the market began its recovery in January of 1975, growing by 65 per cent in just one month. By the end of 1976 it had recovered to pre-oil price crisis levels.

Many investors took years (even decades) to recover from the 1929 Crash and the Great Depression. More recently, Japanese investors are enduring the longest bear market in post war history, with their stock market still 60% below its peak value of eight years ago in 1990.

Other world events, such as the Gulf war, sent stock markets into crisis but the effects were, for the most part, temporary, and, in general, the recovery comparatively fast.

Another lesson that can be learnt from the global stock market crashes is that their effects can be limited by diversification, both across markets and asset types. This reduces the risk of problems in a single market having a major effect on your portfolio of investments.

Always remember that nobody can completely guard against adverse world events which may affect your investment. Because such events are largely unpredictable, the best way to see out the uncertainty of investing is to give it plenty of time.

For readers who ask the question 'When will the next crash happen?' the answer is unknown. If history repeats itself, such events may and probably will happen in the future. But if history really does repeat itself, then quality equity investment is also likely to come through such events and will continue to be the top-performing asset class in the long term.

Part V

tips about making your mind up

This final section attempts to 'pull together' all the advice from earlier chapters and is recommended for all investors.

Chapter 14

Sleeping with your portfolio

The American investment banker, J.P. Morgan, was asked for advice about investing by a friend who was having trouble sleeping because of his stock market investments. His advice was to 'sell down to the sleep level'. Quite simply, the suggestion is that you should only invest in those investments that will not disturb your sleep patterns!

Table 17: 'The Sleeping Point'

Sleeping point	*Investment type*
Deep, restful sleep.	Bank accounts.
Sound sleep.	Term deposits.
Occasional dreams but sound night.	Guaranteed bonds, gilts, savings certs.
Some tossing and turning and possible broken sleep.	Tracker bonds.
Might cause broken sleep occasionally but over the long run you'll be well rested.	Pooled funds.
Broken sleep and more vivid dreams.	Direct stocks and property.
Bouts of insomnia.	Futures, options, commodities.

How risky is the investment?	How long must you invest for?
No risk of losing what you put in.	No specific period.
No risk of losing what you put in.	Usually one to three months minimum to get full returns.
No risk once you stay the term.	Longer-term commitment Two to six years.
No risk to the capital, Returns not secure.	Usually at least three years but more often five/six.
Some ups and downs but long-term performance is generally strong.	Recommended a minimum of five years.
Ups and downs are inevitable with stocks. Rental income not guaranteed.	Longer term holding recommended.
Very risky.	Varies.

CHECKLIST

Chapter 15

Matching your investment strategy to stages in your life cycle

To start with, there are at least three things you should consider when it comes to deciding how you want to invest:

- Are you investing for a short-term objective or for the long term? (See Chapter 2.)
- What stage of life are you at?
- How much risk are you prepared to take?

Let's look at each of these in turn.

Short and longer term objectives

Let's say you have a very specific objective in mind, for example to build up a deposit for a house in, say, two years time. This needs to be funded with specific assets dedicated to that task. You should save with a deposit or other secure instrument. There simply isn't the time to use other investments.

With longer-term objectives such as funding for your retirement, you can aim for greater growth by taking more risks.

What stage of life are you at?

The younger you are the more aggressive you can afford to be with your longer-term investments. In your twenties and thirties there's lots of time to ride out the ups and downs that your investment may go through, as you have a lifetime of earnings in front of you. As many people of this age do not have lump sums to invest, regular investment plans such as PIPs and PEPs may be a suitable way to get started.

As you grow older or as family responsibilities increase, it's generally advisable to cut back on the more risky investments and increase the proportion devoted to more stable investments. By the time you reach your mid-fifties, you should be thinking about the transition to retirement and investing for a replacement income in later years.

How much risk are you prepared to take?

Here's a quick quiz that will give you a sense of the type of investor you are.

Q1. *Your IR£10,000 investment loses 15 per cent of its value in a market correction just one month after you invest. Do you-*

a) sit tight and wait?

b) sell the investment and put it on deposit?

c) invest more in the market?

A:________

Q2. *A month after you invest the value of your investment rockets by 50 per cent. Do you-*

a) cash in?

b) hold, in the expectation of further gains?

c) invest more – it will probably go higher?

A:________

Q3. *Which would you rather have done?*

a) invest in a 100% equity unit-linked fund which grew by very little in six months?

b) place your money in a high interest deposit only to find the 100% equity unit-linked fund doubled in value in six months?

A:__________

Q4. *You are given a choice of the following. Which would you take?*

a) IR£1,000 in cash?

b) a 50% chance of winning IR£4,000?

c) a 20% chance of winning IR£10,000?

d) a 5% chance of winning IR£100,000?

A:__________

Q5. *You have lost IR£50 at the races. How much are you prepared to lose to win the IR£50 back?*

a) nothing – you quit now?

b) IR£10?

c) IR£20?

d) IR£30?

e) IR£40?

A:__________

Your score					
Q1	a) 3	b) 1	c) 5		
Q2	a) 1	b) 3	c) 6		
Q3	a) 3	b) 1			
Q4	a) 1	b) 3	c) 5	d) 9	
Q5	a) 1	b) 2	c) 4	d) 6	e) 8

If you scored...
below 10: You are a conservative investor – stay with sober low-risk investments. Your equity investments should probably be in lower risk vehicles such as tracker bonds.
10–20: You are an active investor and should be well able to take prudent calculated risks. Pooled funds are probably the most appropriate vehicle for your equity investments.
20 or over: You appear to be a risk-taker. Your equity investments can afford to be a bit racier – so perhaps Special Portfolio Investment Accounts may suit, along with more specialist pooled funds.

Life cycle guide to investing

As you go through life, it's generally wise to reduce your exposure to riskier assets. Here's one suggested approach to how a person could mix the various assets that we've talked about in this book.

Age: 30's to 50's

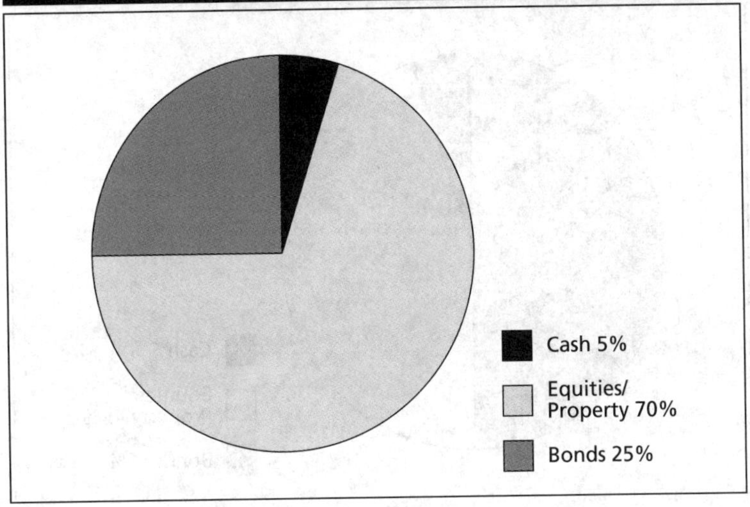

Late 50's to early 60's

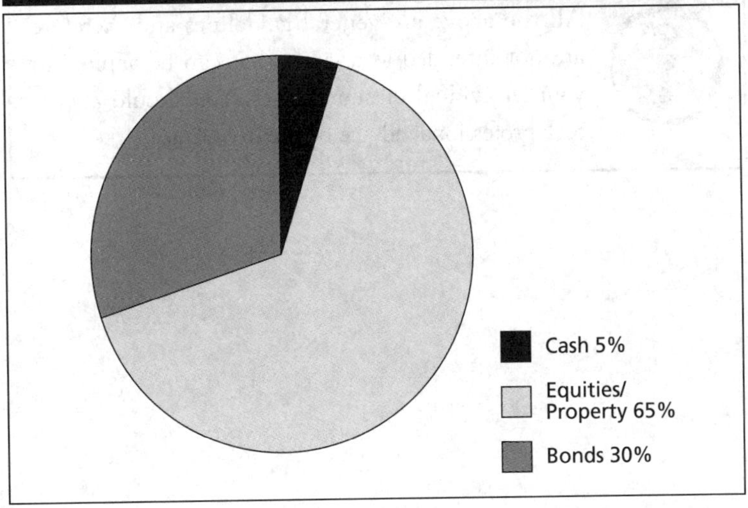

60's plus

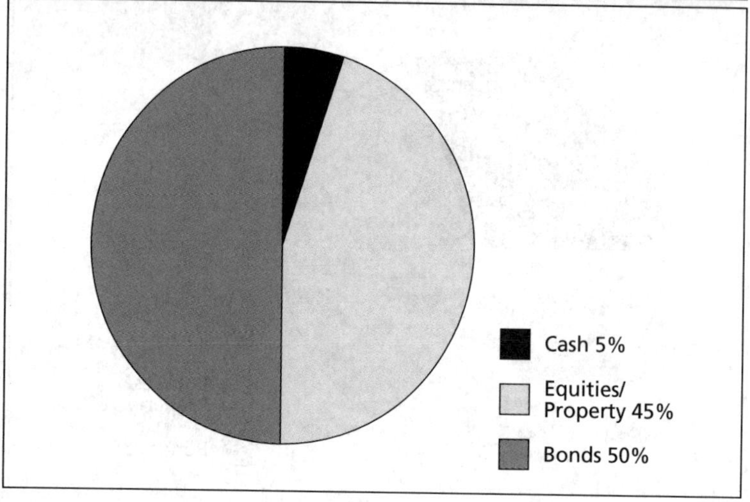

All the above are general guidelines and therefore are not intended as a guide that can be applied to your individual circumstances. You should always seek professional advice before investing.

Europe

Chapter 16

Investing in a country called 'Europe'

What does the future hold for Irish investors?

Deposits and property investments have dominated the Irish investment market for decades. With falling interest rates and strong stock market performance, this pattern has been changing in recent times. The post EMU environment will probably herald the most significant change in Irish investing habits yet. We are likely to see an environment in which:

- interest rates fall as Irish rates converge with continental levels. Rates of interest on deposit are likely to look less attractive.
- tax breaks for property have been eroded in the recent budget and this process may well continue as our tax system harmonises with the rest of Europe.
- long-term investing, especially for pension funding, will become increasingly important.

If we look to the USA, we can get a sense of the types of changes we are likely to see across Europe in the coming years.

In 1980, there were 564 mutual funds in the US and they were worth $135 billion. By 1997, this had jumped to 6,809 funds worth $4.48 trillion. (The equivalent investments in Ireland are the 'pooled investments' we spoke of in an earlier chapter).

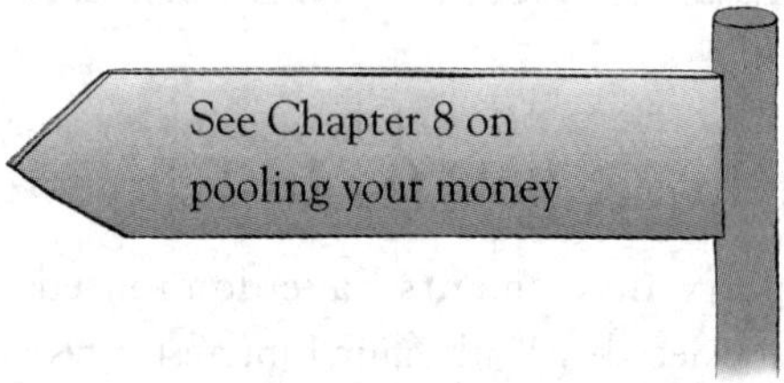

In less than 20 years, Americans, as private individuals, have become massive investors in business and, despite some difficult periods, they have become wealthier by doing so.

Table 18: Facts about US investors
37 million US households invest in one or more mutual funds – total of 63 million individuals.
Nearly half of the new investments that Americans make are in mutual funds.
One survey suggested that 96% of these people accept that their mutual fund investment involves some risk.
Two thirds of US investors invest for a period of five years or more.

Source: Investment Company Institute 1997

The equivalent products in Ireland are those we featured in Chapter 8 and include

- unit trusts
- unit-linked funds
- with-profit bonds

The pattern in Europe is unlikely to replicate this exactly, but it seems very likely that the Irish investor will be investing much more in stock market instruments and in pooled funds in years to come.

This is not the only change that Irish investors are likely to see in the future. It is most likely that there will be a growth in the choice of types of investments available to Irish investors from both Irish and other European institutions. As Irish investors grow in sophistication, we will see the development of many new ways to invest, including by telephone and via the internet.

1
2
3
4
5
6
7
8
9
10

Chapter 17

Ten things to remember about long-term investing

Faced with new choices and ways of investing, it is easy to become confused. To avoid this, stick to some simple guidelines.

1 Maximise your returns within reason

Remember that the one thing you are trying to do is get the maximum total return after taxes, without taking risks that will keep you awake at night.

2 Stay flexible

There is no such thing as a perfect investment and there is certainly no such thing as a permanently perfect investment. Try to be open-minded and flexible but retain a sense of scepticism.

3 Think long-term and stay put

Bull markets are born on pessimism, grow on scepticism, mature on optimism and die on euphoria, so the saying goes. Don't even try to time these, as it is simply not possible to get it right all the time. A far more sound approach is to stick with your investment through the good and bad times.

4 Things change

Bear markets do not last forever. Neither do bull markets. The popularity of particular investments also goes in phases. When you invest, stay invested – that's where the money is, without the white-knuckle ride!

5 Stay critical

Too many investors follow the popular without finding an investment that is suited to their needs. Make up your mind what it is you need from your investment and get advice about how to meet that need.

6 History does repeat

They say that the most costly four words in financial history are 'This time it's different'. There are many lessons to be learnt from the history of investment and they do have a habit of repeating themselves.

7 Keep a cool head

Markets do make significant movements from time to time and the downward ones can be headline-grabbing. History shows that it's worth waiting for markets to recover.

8 Get diversified

There is no way to remove the risk that some investments may go down in value from time to time – it can, does and will happen. However, there is much less chance of a number of different investments doing badly at the same time, particularly if they are in different assets or in different countries. So make sure your investment is well spread around.

9 Keep liquid for everyday needs

Deposits and other short-term securities are an important part of every person's portfolio of assets. Keep as much as you can for your everyday needs in current accounts. Keep your short-term wealth in higher interest bearing accounts. Don't leave your long-term money in short-term deposits. The so-called 'real assets' such as equities and property have delivered better value in the long term and are a better place for your long-term money, in general.

10 No one knows everything about investments

An investment expert who claims to have all the answers doesn't really understand the questions. Watch for those that seem to have surefire ways of making fast returns. Such opportunities are rare. The more returns you are looking to make the greater the risk your investment will have to take, in general.

Published by Bank of Ireland Asset Management,
Ferry House, 48-53 Lower Mount Street,
Dublin 2. Phone (01) 639 9000.

Written by Mark Cunningham, BIAM. Research by Kevin Quinn, BIAM. Data provided courtesy of Software Vineyard and Pat Healy, author of "Pension Fund Investment – a liability based approach", a paper presented to The Society of Actuaries in Ireland, in 1996.

May 1998